Clean Water Timeline

1790 BCE

King Hammurabi of Babylon sets out laws that include punishments for stealing water.

500 CE

First recorded use of a windmill to pump fresh water, in Persia (modern Iran).

1890s

Chlorine begins to be added to purify water supplies.

200 BCE

A medical document in India recommends filtering water to make it cleaner.

1503

Leonardo da Vinci works on a plan to divert the Arno River away from the city of Pisa during its war with Florence.

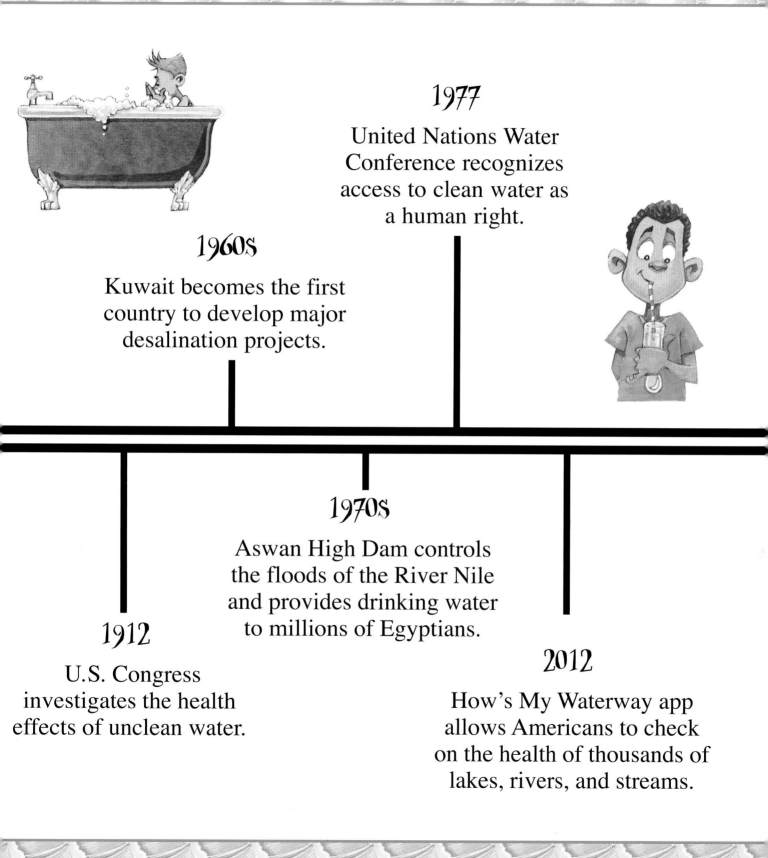

1977

United Nations Water Conference recognizes access to clean water as a human right.

1960s

Kuwait becomes the first country to develop major desalination projects.

1970s

Aswan High Dam controls the floods of the River Nile and provides drinking water to millions of Egyptians.

1912

U.S. Congress investigates the health effects of unclean water.

2012

How's My Waterway app allows Americans to check on the health of thousands of lakes, rivers, and streams.

The Water Cycle

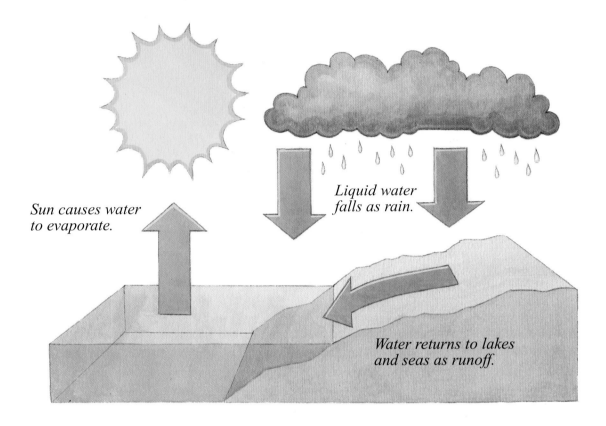

Sun causes water to evaporate.

Liquid water falls as rain.

Water returns to lakes and seas as runoff.

Earth's water is constantly on the move—on, under, and above the ground. This motion is called the water cycle. Warmth from the sun causes water on oceans and lakes to evaporate (become a gas). This gas, called water vapor, enters the air of Earth's atmosphere. As the air cools, the water vapor becomes a liquid again and forms tiny drops inside clouds. These drops join together to form larger drops and eventually fall to the ground as rain. Much of that water becomes runoff, flowing downhill and eventually reaching the ocean... where the cycle begins again.

Author:

Roger Canavan is an accomplished author who has written, edited, and contributed to more than a dozen books about science and other educational subjects. His three children are his sternest critics—and his fellow explorers in the pursuit of knowledge.

Artist:

David Antram was born in Brighton, England, in 1958. He studied at Eastbourne College of Art and then worked in advertising for 15 years before becoming a full-time artist. He has illustrated many children's nonfiction books.

Series creator:

David Salariya was born in Dundee, Scotland. He has illustrated a wide range of books and has created and designed many new series for publishers in the UK and overseas. David established The Salariya Book Company in 1989. He lives in Brighton with his wife, illustrator Shirley Willis, and their son, Jonathan.

Editors: **Caroline Coleman, Stephen Haynes**

Editorial Assistant: **Mark Williams**

PAPER FROM
SUSTAINABLE
FORESTS

Published in Great Britain in 2015 by
The Salariya Book Company Ltd
25 Marlborough Place, Brighton BN1 1UB

ISBN-13: 978-0-531-21219-6 (lib. bdg.) 978-0-531-21310-0 (pbk.)

All rights reserved.
Published in 2015 in the United States
by Franklin Watts
An imprint of Scholastic Inc.
Published simultaneously in Canada.

A CIP catalog record for this book is available
from the Library of Congress.

Printed and bound in Heyuan, China.
Printed on paper from sustainable sources.
Reprinted in MMXIX.
9 10 11 12 13 14 15 R 24 23 22 21 20 19

SCHOLASTIC, FRANKLIN WATTS, and associated logos are trademarks and/or registered trademarks of Scholastic Inc., 557 Broadway, New York, NY 10012.

You Wouldn't Want to Live Without™
Clean Water!

Written by
Roger Canavan

Illustrated by
David Antram

Created and designed by
David Salariya

Franklin Watts®
An Imprint of Scholastic Inc.
NEW YORK • TORONTO • LONDON • AUCKLAND • SYDNEY
MEXICO CITY • NEW DELHI • HONG KONG
DANBURY, CONNECTICUT

Contents

Introduction

Aliens approaching Earth for the first time would see a blue planet in their spaceship's windshield. They'd be right if they guessed that water covered more than two-thirds of the planet. But down here on Earth we know that only about 2 percent of that water is drinkable. That water is necessary—not just for your survival but for the survival of all living things. So it's not just that you wouldn't *want* to live without clean water—you wouldn't be *able* to live without clean water!

It helps you fight against disease, enables you to grow, and even helps you think. And that doesn't even begin to list the ways in which the world needs water to grow things, to build things, and to get them from one place to another. Have some fun while you drink at the fountain. But think about how you'd feel if you turned its handle one day and nothing came out!

Where Does Water Come From?

You might find it fun to splash around in puddles, or maybe you stay awake at night, worrying about whether your picnic will be rained out. Perhaps you're fascinated by maps showing lakes that are as large as some countries, or rivers so wide that you can't see the other side. But have you ever wondered where all that water comes from, or where it goes? Who knows whether yesterday's thunderstorm contained water that flowed down the River Nile last year, or maybe in the time of the Pharaohs? Just how do we track this precious natural resource?

It'll dry up in a month or so!

An Endless Journey

THE JOURNEY that water makes from sky to land to sea and back again is called the water cycle. Heat and gravity act on water to keep it moving constantly. We can divert water for our own use along the way, but it tends to find its way back into the cycle.

CHANGES IN TEMPERATURE and air pressure cause tiny water droplets to come together to form larger drops inside clouds. These fall to the earth as rain.

SOME RAINWATER seeps into the ground but much of it, called runoff, spills downhill, forming streams and rivers as it flows toward the sea.

RESERVOIRS are large man-made lakes that collect fresh water for cities and towns. Dams on the edge of these reservoirs control the flow of water.

You Can Do It!

Make your own weather! Place a cup in a mixing bowl. Pour water into the bowl (not the cup) so that it's about two fingers deep. Stretch plastic wrap across the top of the bowl and place a small weight on the film, just above the cup. Rest the bowl on a sunny windowsill and in a couple of days you'll see that water has "rained" into the cup.

PUMPS USE PRESSURE to force water up from underground. Small hand pumps are sometimes enough to suit the needs of a family.

TREES AND OTHER PLANTS also search for water underground. Their roots contain tiny tubes that draw water up into every part of the plant.

WATER EVAPORATES, or changes from liquid to gas form, when it is exposed to heat or wind. This invisible gas, called water vapor, remains in the air.

CONDENSATION. Air can hold a lot of water, either invisibly or in the clouds. This water condenses—becomes liquid again—when it cools.

How Long Could You Go Without Water?

Did you know that almost two-thirds of your body weight is water? Water is pretty much everywhere inside you—helping to keep you nourished, flushing away waste, and generally keeping you healthy. You could survive far longer without food than you could without water. Emergency services rush to find survivors after earthquakes and other disasters because they are concerned about getting water to those people. Being dehydrated (running low on water) is dangerous, and you really need to drink water before you become thirsty.

Heating and Cooling

SWEAT (mainly water) evaporates on your skin, taking heat away as the water turns to vapor. When your body warms itself by shivering, your pores close to keep heat and moisture in.

YOU SHOULD DRINK WATER regularly throughout the day to hydrate (help your body maintain its supply of water, which is constantly being used up).

Ugh!

YOUR IMMUNE SYSTEM, which fights disease and infection, relies on water to keep you healthy—or to help you recover from illness.

Top Tip

Go easy on the salt. Your body balances the water and salt inside you. If you sweat, you need to take in more of both. The salt in a sports drink draws water from your stomach to muscles and other areas. But if you eat something salty without drinking, the salt in your stomach draws water back from other parts of your body.

YOUR BODY uses lots of water to digest (break down) food so that it can extract what's needed for health and growth.

ONCE THE NUTRITIOUS PARTS have been extracted, water helps your body get rid of waste (the parts that it doesn't need).

NO ONE WANTS to run out of water in the desert! The intense heat and lack of shade cause your body to lose even more water—as sweat—as you search for clean water to drink. In really hot conditions, you would need to find water within two days.

9

How Does Clean Water Keep You Healthy?

We use water in many ways, and in many of these uses it's important for the water to be clean. Of course, the water you drink needs to be free of germs in order for you to avoid illness.

But water itself can also help you to ward off infection. You use water to wash or rinse away germs that could be harmful. Doctors and nurses need water to wash their hands before treating patients so that they don't transfer germs to them.

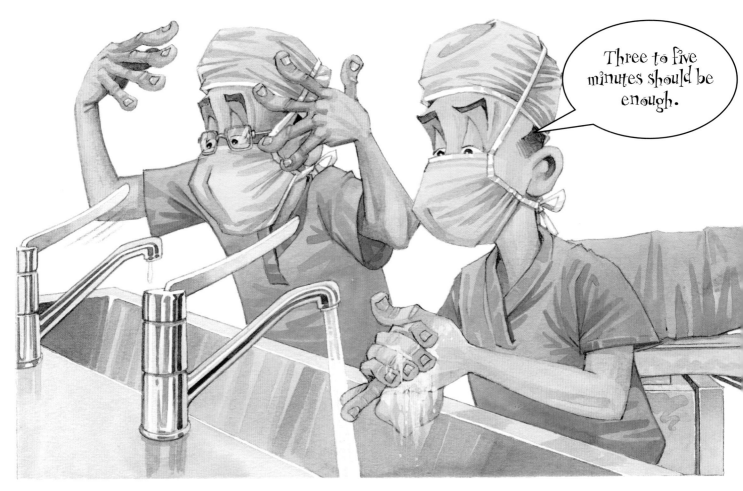

STAYING CLEAN does more than just help us to feel good. Washing well and then rinsing with clean water is an important part of personal hygiene.

TREATING WOUNDS. The first step in treating any wound is to clean it with pure water to remove anything that might interfere with healing.

Top Tip

Bits of food can stick to your teeth, or between them, after you've finished eating. Acids form when these bits mix with plaque (a sticky substance on the teeth). Those acids eat away at your teeth. Regular brushing—which includes a good rinsing with water—washes away this harmful acid.

SEWERS REMOVE WASTE from towns and cities just as toilets remove waste from your house. Harmful substances flow away in the water.

HYDROTHERAPY is a form of medicine that uses water (*hydor* in Greek) for pain relief—for both humans and animals.

HIS LIFE IS IN THEIR HANDS. Surgeons carry an enormous responsibility in any medical operation. Before they touch a single instrument, they scrub their hands and forearms with a special solution and rinse with clean water to make sure they aren't carrying any infection themselves.

Can Dirty Water Make You Sick?

*J*ust as clean water keeps you healthy and helps you grow, dirty water can make you unhealthy and sick. Water can contain tiny organisms and even poisons that cause disease. Our understanding of these diseases—and their link with water—has grown over time. But no matter how advanced the modern methods of treating these diseases, doctors insist that the best prevention is to make sure that everyone has supplies of clean water.

PLAYING IN DIRTY WATER might seem like fun, until you begin to feel sick.

Milestones

400 BCE Hippocrates claims that many diseases are linked to water.
1340s CE Europeans blame "bad air" for deaths from waterborne diseases.
1670 Antonie van Leeuwenhoek improves the microscope; 13 years later, he discovers bacteria.
1849 William Budd claims that cholera is caused by microorganisms that travel in water.
1854 John Snow uses statistics to help discover the source of a cholera outbreak.
1857 Louis Pasteur observes that many diseases are caused by germs.
1882 Robert Koch proves that many diseases are transmitted through water.
1907 Water filtering in Lawrence, Massachusetts, reduces death rate from typhoid fever by 79 percent.

Water and Disease

GIARDIASIS is an infection of the digestive system caused by tiny parasites that live in water. It leads to bad stomach pains and diarrhea.

OTITIS EXTERNA, sometimes called swimmer's ear, leads to pain and swelling in the ear. It's caused by bacteria and fungi in dirty water.

Top Tip

Before you visit a foreign country, ask a medical professional whether it's safe to drink the water there. You might need to boil water before drinking it to kill germs and prevent the spread of infection.

THE BROAD STREET PUMP. Doctor John Snow blamed infected water (not "bad air") for London's deadly outbreak of cholera in 1854. He had the handle of the public water pump in Broad Street, where many people had died, removed. The outbreak soon faded away. The pump had been dug only 3 feet (1 meter) from an old cesspit.

Right you are, governor.

HEPATITIS A, often caused by viruses in water supplies, leads to tiredness, nausea (feeling that you're going to throw up), and weight loss.

Cough!

THE FLU (short for "influenza") is a viral infection that's like a much more serious common cold. Thorough hand-washing can prevent its spread.

Do Animals and Plants Need Clean Water?

Water is essential for life, and not just for us humans. All living creatures—plants, animals, and even the tiniest microorganisms—depend on clean water for their survival. Just like us, they become thirsty and need to find water in their environment. Some need to live in it, others need to drink lots of it. Still others seem to survive without it, but when you look more closely you find that even they have ways of finding and storing the water that they need.

That's a plant with attitude!

MANY DESERT PLANTS, such as this cactus, have thick, fleshy stems that store water over long periods with no rain. Sharp needles keep animals from eating these plants.

WATER-LILY LEAVES float on the surface, with stems leading down to roots on the lake bed. Some leaves are large enough to hold a child.

A PADDY is a flooded field where rice is grown and harvested. Its name comes from the Malay word *padi*, which simply means "rice." Unlike many plants, rice can grow in very wet areas. Water also protects the rice from weeds and many insect pests.

You Can Do It!

See for yourself how plants suck up water through their stems, just like drinking with a straw. Put a carnation in a clear vase or bottle of water. Add about 10 drops of food coloring and wait a day for the flower to change color.

GRIZZLY BEARS scoop up salmon as they swim up rivers. When rivers become polluted, these bears and other fish-eaters must roam much farther to find their next meal—because salmon need clean water to survive.

CAMELS can go for long periods without water, but when they do drink they fill up quickly.

KOALAS never seem to leave their comfortable perches in Australia's eucalyptus trees to come down and drink. But koalas do need water, and they get it by chewing eucalyptus leaves.

Does It Matter How Much You Use?

Have you ever thought about how much water you use each day and how much of that is just wasted? True, water finds its way back into the air and clouds, but a lot of waste water becomes contaminated by chemicals. And then it's hard to replace the water that's gone "down the drain."

splash!

Many people have now realized that conservation starts at home. If everyone did their part, then more clean water would be there for those who really need it. Are you really watering your lawn—or is the street getting most of that precious water? It can be fun to find ways of saving water that still let you live normally.

SHOWERING for five minutes, instead of ten, can save about 30 gallons (113.5 liters) of water—that's still enough time for a good song.

WASHING DISHES by filling the sink with water, rather than having the faucet run nonstop, saves more than 20 gallons (76 L) of water.

LEAVING A HOSE RUNNING while you wash your car is a big waste of water—about 120 gallons (454 L) down the drain.

A SMALL REPAIR to a toilet can stop it from "running all the time" and wasting up to 300 gallons (1,136 L) of water a day.

17

How Far Could You Carry a Bucket of Water?

You just turn on a faucet to get water. But in the past—and in many places today—the nearest water might be far away. You'd need to carry it a long way, unless you could find an easier way of getting it to where it's needed. Some ancient Roman aqueducts (long pipes or channels to carry water) still work after 2,000 years!

Milestones

6500 BCE Wells are dug to supply fresh water in what is now Israel.

2500 BCE Public water supply and indoor plumbing are developed in India.

1500 BCE Cumbe Mayo aqueduct is built high in the Peruvian Andes.

312 BCE Romans begin building their first aqueduct.

1325 CE Monks build a pipeline into Cambridge, England, from a spring outside the city.

1613 The New River connects 20 miles (32 km) of wells and springs as a man-made river supplying London.

1729 San Antonio River is diverted to irrigate farms in Texas.

1801 Philadelphia, Pennsylvania, becomes the first U.S. city to use steam pumps to supply water.

1914 U.S. government establishes standards for drinking water on ships, trains, and other interstate carriers.

WELLS (right) are built above underground water. Some wells are hundreds of feet deep.

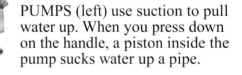

PUMPS (left) use suction to pull water up. When you press down on the handle, a piston inside the pump sucks water up a pipe.

AQUEDUCTS have been around since ancient Roman times. A modern version stretches more than 300 miles (500 kilometers) across the Arizona desert.

DESALINATION, or removing the salt from seawater, is possible—but it takes a lot of expensive equipment (right) to produce fresh water in the end.

Modern

Roman

Lever

A SHADOOF uses the principle of the lever to swing buckets of water from a river back to shore. Egyptians have used shadoofs for more than 3,000 years.

The weight on the other end makes it easier than it looks.

You Can Do It!

Aqueducts rely on a familiar force to move water—gravity. You can build your own aqueduct by running a length of hose across stacks of books. It will only work if the hose goes downhill all the way.

Fulcrum (pivot)

Counterweight

Bucket

19

How Big Is Your Water Footprint?

Water has many other uses besides drinking and washing. It's needed to grow crops, harvest them, build things, transport goods, and fulfill lots of other uses that we never even think about. The United Nations says "we're all downstream," which means that everything around us has used up water somewhere—and maybe we're causing other regions to go without water as a result. Your "water footprint" is a measure of how much water you really use, especially all that water that you don't *see* being used.

6,100 gallons (23,000 L)

A POUND OF STEAK needs a whopping 1,952 gallons (7,389 L) of water to make the long journey from cattle ranch to dinner plate.

THAT MORNING COFFEE that your mom loves used up 39 gallons (148 L) of water to reach her—from coffee plants to coffee cup.

JUST ONE SMALL glass of fruit juice took 32 gallons (121 L) of water to reach the kitchen—just think of pressing, bottling, transporting, and other stages.

EVEN CHICKEN needs a lot of water to reach you—491 gallons (1,859 L) for every pound, unless you live on a chicken farm!

No one will notice...

Top Tip

Thinking about "what's downstream" also means not burying problems that will turn up later, or somewhere else. Just 1 gallon (3.8 L) of diesel fuel pumped underground, for example, can contaminate 1 million gallons (3.8 million L) of clean water underground.

TWO PAIRS of jeans need 6,100 gallons (23,091 L) of water to be produced—enough to fill that huge water tanker behind those children.

THAT COTTON SHIRT might seem a little small, but it still used up 748 gallons (2,831 L) of water to travel from cotton fields to coat hanger.

MOST SPAGHETTI is made from wheat, and a pound of it needs 164 gallons (620 L) of water to get it from the farm to the factory and then to your twirling fork.

YOU MIGHT BE SURPRISED to learn that a single sheet of paper uses 2.8 gallons (10.6 L) of water to go all the way from the tree to your printer.

The Growing Footprint

DIP A CUP into a stream, and the water footprint is just one cup. But to produce a shirt, water is needed to grow cotton plants, carry them to a factory, process them to make thread, weave the thread into cloth, dye it…And with the water needed at every stage, that footprint gets bigger and bigger!

21

How Does That Water Get Used?

Think of some of the ways that you use water—washing, drinking, cooking, swimming, and watering your garden. All of those are important, and together they're described as domestic or household water use. But domestic use only accounts for about one-tenth of the water that's used worldwide. About 70 percent of water use goes into agriculture, helping essential crops and livestock supply our needs.

HUGE COOLING TOWERS rise above electricity power stations, using water to lower the dangerously high temperatures inside.

IN FACTORIES like the one pictured on the left, engineers use color-coded plans to identify which pipes carry hot or cold water.

That explains why things like fruit juice and steak have such a large water footprint. Industry uses another 20 percent, still double the amount used by the world's population of more than 7 billion. Just about anything that's made or used—from basketballs to the Internet—needs clean water. In addition to containing harmful or even poisonous elements, dirty water might have high concentrations of salt, calcium, or other minerals that can form deposits on machinery, making it unusable.

You Can Do It!

You may think that you don't really need that much water—a few drinks, a shower, and that's it. But water is probably being used in your home even as you read this. Try making a list of all the things around you that use or need water.

PUBLIC WATER SUPPLIES into big towns and cities run for many miles from reservoirs to houses, schools, and other buildings.

INDUSTRY needs water at nearly every stage of making things. Most of that water needs to be clean so that it doesn't damage the machinery.

IRRIGATION (supplying water to plants to help them grow) uses up much of the world's water.

Can You Make Dirty Water Clean?

nly 2 percent of Earth's water is drinkable. The rest is either seawater or locked in ice sheets and glaciers (frozen rivers high up in mountains). For many years, humans have been ruining this precious supply of water. Even today, when people are more aware of pollution, about 2 million tons of human waste gets dumped into fresh water every day. Scientists are working hard to turn things around, developing new ways to clean rivers and lakes that had once seemed lost forever. But will they be able to meet the challenges of a world population that's growing at a rate of 230,000 people each day?

Untreated water

Filtered water

FILTERING out small particles is one way to clean water. This system (right) passes water through charcoal. Bits and pieces get caught in the charcoal, and the water flowing out is much cleaner.

Charcoal

REMOVING THE SOURCE of the pollution sometimes involves dealing with dangerous chemicals, which calls for special safety equipment.

A LOW-TECH WAY of cleaning up water is simply to fish objects out of it (right).

AN ADVANCED but natural cleanup technique involves growing tiny organisms called algae in water that has been polluted by chemicals. The algae take in some of the chemicals that have made the water dirty.

Algae

Polluted water

BURNING FAILURE, GLOWING SUCCESS.
Cleveland, Ohio, 1969:
Industrial waste that had been dumped in the Cuyahoga River caught fire. It was a bad event that led to a good outcome. Mayor Carl Stokes persuaded the U.S. government to get involved in cleaning up the river, and his efforts helped lead to the Clean Water Act of 1972. Apartments and restaurants now line the banks of the much-cleaner Cuyahoga River.

How It Works

To see how a simple filter works, use string or a rubber band to tighten an old dish towel across the top of a jar. Pour a glass of muddy water through the cloth into the jar. The cloth filters out lots of material and the water that comes out is cleaner—but it's still not clean enough to drink.

There used to be fish here once.

Milestones

1804 Robert Thom of Scotland builds the first water-treatment plant.

1806 Paris becomes the first major city with a water-treatment policy.

1847 British law makes it a crime to pollute drinking-water supplies.

1855 Chicago becomes the first U.S. city with a planned sewage system.

1890 Methods to treat sewage with bacteria are developed in the United States and Britain.

1961 Wildlife deaths linked to water pollution along the Colorado River in the southwest United States create public anger.

1970 Environmental Protection Agency is set up in the United States.

1980 Michigan-born Verna Mize wins a 13-year battle to stop the Reserve Mining Company from polluting Lake Superior.

2011 Once heavily polluted, the Tyne is named England's best river for salmon.

Would You Go to War Over Water?

You've probably argued with someone in your family about who should have the last doughnut or slice of pizza. Now imagine that you're in charge of a city or a country and that your neighbor is hogging something precious that you feel you should share. You'd feel pretty angry.

Over the past 60 years, countries have often gone to war over oil. Many experts believe that water will be the "oil" of the 21st century—a precious natural resource that could trigger wars. Regardless of who's right and who's wrong in these disputes, the real losers will always be innocent people who have to go without water because of the fighting.

DRY, CRACKED SOIL is all that remains of a field that once produced valuable crops. Countries have gone to war to protect their water supplies.

SWIMMING and other forms of water fun would be out of the question if your country were involved in a water dispute. Water would be reserved for urgent uses.

PEOPLE AFFECTED by fighting often have to walk long distances to reach military checkpoints, where they might find supplies of water.

FARMERS and their livestock are often displaced by fighting, especially if their traditional grazing lands have become dry, or, even worse, dangerous battlefields.

Did You Leave the Water Running?

With all the strain on supplies of clean water, from the world's growing population to the demands of farms and factories, is there any hope for the future? Will we run out? How can you be sure that clean water will come out when your own children or grandchildren turn on the faucet?

Luckily, people have been looking for solutions for years. International organizations try to teach people who have clean water how to save it, so that the thirstiest people get a share of it. Inventors come up with ways—some simple, others like science fiction—to trap or transport water. In the future, there might even be human settlements on other planets, and we might find water trapped beneath their surfaces.

AN ICE CUBE TO GO, and hold the soda. The idea isn't so crazy. Engineers are working on ways to tow giant icebergs from cold regions to drier parts of the world.

SIMPLE MESH SCREENS (right) can trap the water in fog, which is really low-level clouds. Drops collect on the screens, then drip down into containers below.

RAIN BARRELS (left) are back in fashion. They catch and store rainwater, usually for watering garden plants.

CITIES OF THE FUTURE will need to be sustainable, built with conservation in mind. Houses and apartments will save and reuse most of their water. This rooftop garden provides shade and insulation.

You Can Do It!

Consider using solar-powered pumps. They help farmers in parts of northern Kenya to use water that's trapped underground. Some parts of the country have gone for five years without any rain—but all that sunshine can now bring water!

Another giant step for mankind!

Glossary

agriculture Farming, including growing crops and raising livestock.

algae Seaweed and similar organisms.

bacteria Tiny, one-celled microorganisms; some help us to stay healthy, while others carry disease.

cesspit An open hole where human waste is dumped.

cholera A deadly disease caused by bacteria that are carried in dirty water.

condense To change from a gas to a liquid, as water vapor condenses to become drops of liquid water in clouds.

conservation Taking care of the natural world to preserve the wide variety of plants and animals on the planet.

contaminate To make a clean thing dirty or poisonous.

diesel A form of motor fuel that is produced from oil.

element A pure substance, such as gold or oxygen, that is made up of one type of atom (the basic particle of all matter).

environment The natural world, either as a whole (all of the plants, animals, and landscape), or in a particular area.

fungi Types of organisms that are neither plants, animals, nor bacteria. Yeast and mushrooms are types of fungi.

germ A general term to describe bacteria, viruses, and other tiny organisms.

hygiene The actions taken to keep oneself clean.

infection An invasion of the body by organisms that cause disease.

insulation Protection from too much heat or cold.

lever A simple machine that uses a pole or beam to transfer energy, making it easier to move objects. A seesaw is a kind of lever.

livestock Farm animals.

microorganism Any organism that is too small to see without a microscope.

organism Any kind of living thing.

parasite An organism that lives on another organism and harms its "host" by carrying disease or taking its food.

particles Tiny pieces of matter.

pharaohs The rulers of ancient Egypt.

pollute To make something (such as water or air) dirty or unhealthy.

resource Any useful thing that is naturally found in a particular area, such as fresh water, oil, or certain plants and animals.

runoff Water that runs from high ground into streams and rivers.

sewage Human waste that is flushed away from homes or other buildings.

solar Having to do with the sun.

statistics The collection and study of information (usually in the form of numbers) to make sense of what has been observed.

suction The flow of a liquid or gas from an area of high pressure into one of low pressure.

typhoid fever A severe, and often deadly, infection caused by bacteria in unclean water.

United Nations An international organization to promote peace, health, and development around the world.

viruses Tiny organisms that resemble bacteria but cannot reproduce by themselves. Viruses infect cells in other organisms and only reproduce when the infected cells reproduce.

waterborne Transported by or in water.

Index

Preserving Clean Water

Scientists have been warning the public about preserving clean water supplies for decades. The world has acted on many of those warnings, especially the calls to clean up rivers and lakes. Horrible events, such as dead fish washing up on shore or rivers catching fire, have prompted action from many governments.

Educating people about problems that might, or probably will, occur is a good first step to involving the public. For example, people should be taught that watering their lawn or a golf course 24/7 will cause problems somewhere down the line.

Another thing to be aware of is that the world is warming up, partly because of human activity. Called climate change or global warming, the result is the same: We're beginning to see changes in the weather. Some people even talk of a future where Kansas and Oklahoma will be as dry as Arizona is now.

Projects to free up more water for the future are being funded by some of the driest countries on Earth, because they are also some of the richest. The countries near the Persian Gulf, for example, sit above huge deposits of oil. This oil has earned these countries trillions of dollars in the past 40 years.

In 1975, Prince Mohammed Al-Faisal of Saudi Arabia asked French engineer Georges Mougin to consider towing a huge iceberg to the Red Sea from either Greenland or Antarctica. Mougin worked for six years on the project before deciding that it would be too expensive. But in 2009 he returned to it, using advanced computer designs to reduce costs. Perhaps someday an iceberg really will wind up parked by the deserts of the Middle East.

Fresh Water From Seawater

Desalination—removing the salt from salt water—is another costly technique, but it could help a lot of places if costs come down. The cost comes from the complicated equipment needed. There have been some successes with desalination. Dubai, an oil-rich city on the Persian Gulf, now gets 98 percent of its water this way.

Apart from the cost, desalination has another big drawback. What happens to all the salt that is removed from the salt water? It has to go somewhere, but if it's pumped back into the sea it could kill fish and other wildlife.

Maybe one day there will be new, more affordable techniques to help the world save water for current and future generations.

Top Ten Water-Using Countries

(Amount used by each person in a year)

1. United States	479,000 gallons	(1.8 million L)
2. Canada	393,000 gallons	(1.5 million L)
3. Australia	258,000 gallons	(977,000 L)
4. Italy	202,000 gallons	(765,000 L)
5. France	155,000 gallons	(587,000 L)
6. Germany	119,000 gallons	(450,000 L)
7. Switzerland	97,000 gallons	(367,000 L)
8. Sweden	83,000 gallons	(314,000 L)
9. England and Wales	69,000 gallons	(261,000 L)
10. Denmark	33,000 gallons	(125,000 L)

Did You Know?

When one inch (2.5 cm) of rain falls on one acre (0.4 ha) of farmland, it provides more than 27,000 gallons (102,200 L) of water—at no cost to the farmer.

Stretched end to end, the water pipes in the United States and Canada would circle Earth 40 times.

- Parts of the Cloaca Maxima, a sewer built in ancient Rome 2,600 years ago, are still in use today.

- The water found in lakes, rivers, streams, and ponds makes up only 0.3 percent of Earth's fresh water. The rest is locked in ice or is underground.